THERE WAS A BLACK HOLE THAT SWALLOWED THE UNIVERSE

Words by
CHRIS FERRIE

Pictures by
SUSAN BATORI

sourcebooks
eXplore

DEDICATED TO SAGITTARIUS A*,
MY FAVORITE BLACK HOLE.
—CF

TO ROBERT, WHO IS MY SHINING STAR
AND LIGHTS MY WAY WHEREVER I GO.
—SB

Text © 2019, 2021 by Chris Ferrie
Illustrations by Susan Batori
Cover and internal design and illustrations © 2019, 2021 by Sourcebooks
Sourcebooks and the colophon are registered trademarks of Sourcebooks.
All rights reserved.
This book is a parody and has not been prepared, approved, or authorized by the creators
of "There Was an Old Lady Who Swallowed a Fly" or their heirs or representatives.
The full color art was first sketched, then painted digitally using a variety of brushes and textures in Photoshop.
Published by Sourcebooks eXplore, an imprint of Sourcebooks Kids
P.O. Box 4410, Naperville, Illinois 60567-4410
(630) 961-3900
sourcebookskids.com
Library of Congress Cataloging-in-Publication Data is on file with the publisher.
Source of Production: Wing King Tong Paper Products Co. Ltd., Shenzhen, Guangdong Province, China
Date of Production: April 2021
Run Number: 5021603
Printed and bound in China.
WKT 10 9 8 7 6 5 4 3 2 1

There was a BLACK HOLE that swallowed the UNIVERSE.

I don't know why it swallowed the universe
—oh well, it couldn't get WORSE.

There was a BLACK HOLE that swallowed a GALAXY.
It left quite a cavity after swallowing that galaxy.

It swallowed the GALAXIES
that filled the UNIVERSE.

I don't know why it swallowed the universe
—oh well, it couldn't get WORSE.

There was a BLACK HOLE that swallowed a STAR.

It couldn't get far, that bright shining star.

It swallowed the STARS that lit up the GALAXIES.
It swallowed the GALAXIES that filled the UNIVERSE.

I don't know why it swallowed the universe
—oh well, it couldn't get WORSE.

There was a BLACK HOLE that swallowed a PLANET.

Very organic, this fine-looking planet.

It swallowed the PLANETS that orbited STARS.
It swallowed the STARS that lit up the GALAXIES.
It swallowed the GALAXIES that filled the UNIVERSE.

I don't know why it swallowed the universe
—oh well, it couldn't get **WORSE.**

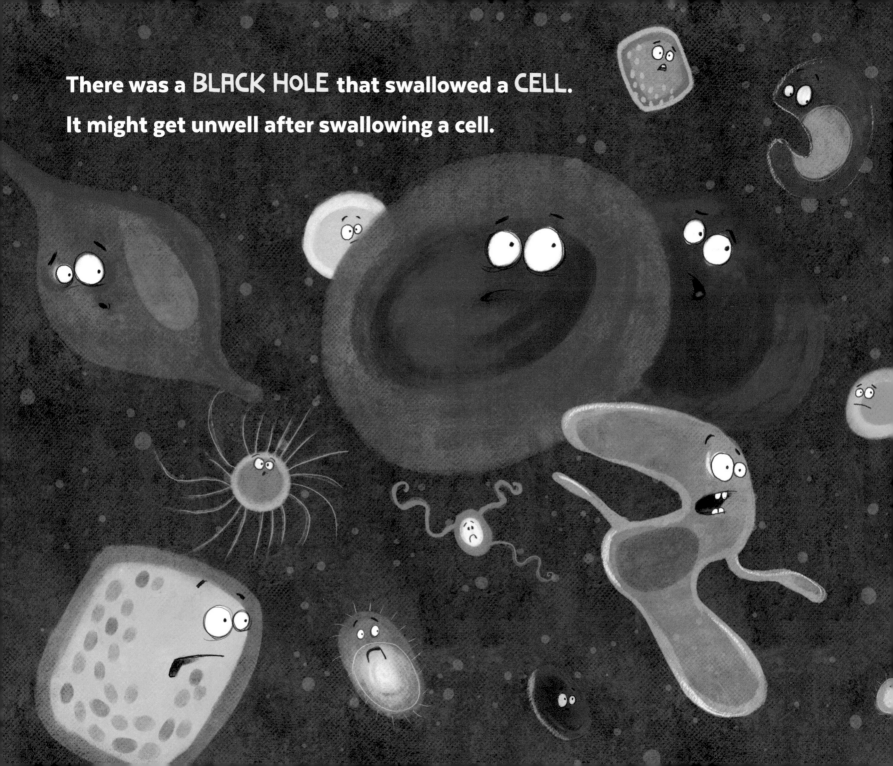

There was a BLACK HOLE that swallowed a CELL.
It might get unwell after swallowing a cell.

It swallowed the CELLS that gave life to the PLANETS.

It swallowed the PLANETS that orbited STARS.

It swallowed the STARS that lit up the GALAXIES.

It swallowed the GALAXIES that filled the UNIVERSE.

I don't know why it swallowed the universe
—oh well, it couldn't get WORSE.

There was a BLACK HOLE that swallowed a MOLECULE.
It thought it was fuel, a big molecule.

It swallowed the MOLECULES that fed the CELLS.

It swallowed the CELLS that gave life to the PLANETS.

It swallowed the PLANETS that orbited STARS.

It swallowed the STARS that lit up the GALAXIES.

It swallowed the GALAXIES that filled the UNIVERSE.

I don't know why it swallowed the universe
—oh well, it couldn't get WORSE.

There was a BLACK HOLE that swallowed an ATOM.

It's hard to get at 'em, those tiny atoms.

It swallowed the ATOMS that built up the MOLECULES.

It swallowed the MOLECULES that fed the CELLS.

It swallowed the CELLS that gave life to the PLANETS.

It swallowed the PLANETS that orbited STARS.

It swallowed the STARS that lit up the GALAXIES.

It swallowed the GALAXIES that filled the UNIVERSE.

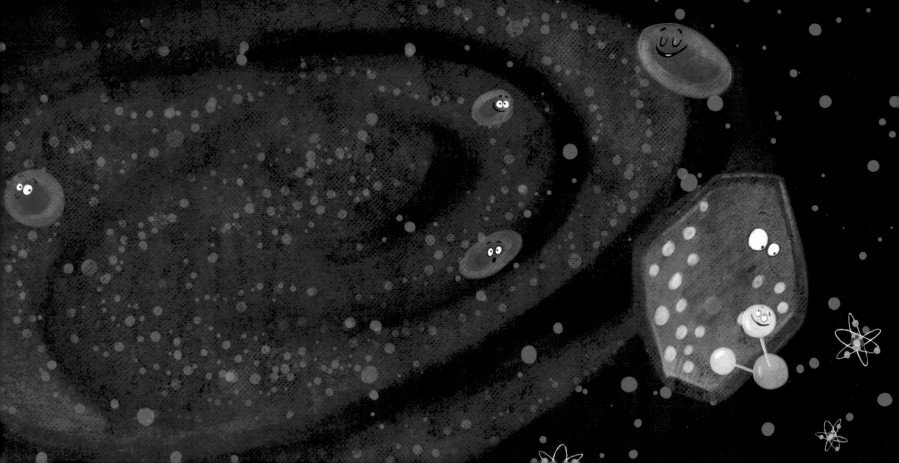

I don't know why it swallowed the universe

—oh well, it couldn't get WORSE.

There was a BLACK HOLE that swallowed a NEUTRON.

A good start to build on, a neutral neutron.

It swallowed the NEUTRONS that stabled the ATOMS.

It swallowed the ATOMS that built up the MOLECULES.

It swallowed the MOLECULES that fed the CELLS.

It swallowed the CELLS that gave life to the PLANETS.

It swallowed the PLANETS that orbited STARS.

It swallowed the STARS that lit up the GALAXIES.

It swallowed the GALAXIES that filled the UNIVERSE.

I don't know why it swallowed the universe
—oh well, it couldn't get WORSE.

There was a **BLACK HOLE** that swallowed a **QUARK.**

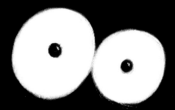

That's all there was.

And now it's DARK.

STELLAR BLACK HOLE FACTS

YOU CAN'T SEE A BLACK HOLE BECAUSE IT DOESN'T REFLECT LIGHT. IT ACTUALLY PULLS LIGHT IN WITH ITS IMMENSE GRAVITY!

THE PLACE BEYOND WHICH NOTHING CAN ESCAPE A BLACK HOLE IS CALLED THE EVENT HORIZON.

THE CENTER OF THE BLACK HOLE IS CALLED THE SINGULARITY. WE MIGHT NEVER KNOW WHAT HAPPENS THERE.

BLACK HOLES WARP SPACE AND TIME AROUND THEM. TO US, TIME APPEARS TO MOVE MUCH SLOWER NEAR A BLACK HOLE.

WHEN TWO BLACK HOLES COLLIDE, THEY SEND OUT WAVES OF ENERGY THAT STRETCH AND SQUISH SPACE ITSELF!

SCIENTISTS BELIEVE THERE IS A HUGE BLACK HOLE AT THE CENTER OF EVERY SPIRAL GALAXY, INCLUDING OUR OWN MILKY WAY!